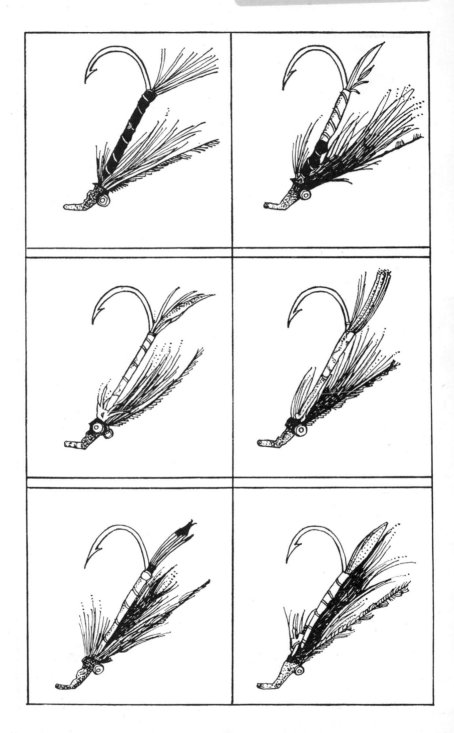

MACDONALD JUNIOR REFERENCE LIBRARY

FISHING

JRL 54

MACDONALD JUNIOR REFERENCE LIBRARY

FISHING

MACDONALD EDUCATIONAL
49–50 POLAND STREET, LONDON W.1.

Editor's Note

This book gives an account of fishing as a sport and of the equipment and methods that fishermen use. It describes the types, surroundings and habits of the fish that are commonly caught in sea and fresh water. Fish as part of the animal kingdom are dealt with in the book *Fishes*, in this series, and their evolution is described in the book *Prehistoric Life*, also in this series.

Contents

The History of Fishing

The earliest fishermen were prehistoric men. We know that they were able to catch fish because some bone hooks have been found that are about 50,000 years old. Very simple fishing tackle is still used by tribes in many parts of the world. The first time fishing was mentioned in writing was two thousand years ago. There is a manuscript, written in Anglo-Saxon and Latin, in which a fisherman describes how he caught Eels, Pike, Minnows, Trout 'and whatever else swims in the river'. The first people interested in fishing for its own sake were probably monks. They kept fish in ponds, which were called stew ponds. A prioress probably wrote the first English work on fishing, printed in 1496. Since that time very many books have been written about fishing, because it has become a popular sport in many countries. The most famous book on fishing was written by Izaak Walton in 1653. It is called *The Compleat Angler*. Fishing methods have changed a great deal since Izaak Walton's day, but his book can still be read for pleasure. Today there are more fishermen than ever before. Wastes from factories have poisoned or polluted many rivers so that fish no longer live in them. During the last 50 years, fishermen have realized that their sport may be in danger. Clubs have been organized which help look after rivers and lakes by restocking them with fish. These clubs try to make sure that pollution does not occur.

At the end of the day the fisherman can take pride in his catch. His skill has provided his family with a tasty dinner.

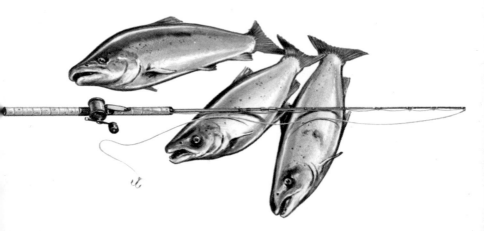

Places where Fish are Caught

There are two main groups of fish : *salt-water* or *marine* fish, and *fresh-water* fish. Salt-water fish live in the sea. Fresh-water fish live in rivers, streams, ponds and lakes. There are a few fish which live in both fresh water and the sea. These can be caught in estuaries. An *estuary* is the mouth of a river where it flows into the sea. Some, like the Salmon, are *migratory* — that is, they are born in rivers but spend most of their lives in the sea, returning to the rivers to spawn.

There are three groups of sea fish, depending on where they feed. The first group feed on or near the sea bottom. These fish are called *bottom feeders.* The second group consists of fish that feed somewhere between the sea bottom and the surface. These fish are called *mid-water feeders*. Finally there are fish that live near the surface of the sea, and they are called *surface feeders.* The sea fisherman is able to fish from a boat or from the shore. If he has a boat, the fisherman can catch surface-feeding fish, mid-water fish and bottom-feeding fish. He can fish from a few hundred yards from the shore to many miles out to sea. The shore fisherman catches fish that live just off sandy beaches or along rocky shores. Sea fish can also be caught from piers. In the sea,

Fresh-water fishing is one of the most peaceful of sports.

Sea-fishing is often a dramatic and exciting sport.

the exact position of the fish varies with the tides and seasons. Shoals of fish often come close to the shore at high tide, and swim out again at low tide.

Fresh-water fish are caught in rivers, streams, canals, ponds and lakes. River fish are of two main kinds: those that prefer fast-flowing rivers, and those that live in slow rivers. Some fish can be caught in streams so narrow that you can jump over them.

Catching fish depends on knowing when and where fish feed. Some fish stay in the same place all the time, but others move from place to place. Because conditions in the river vary from season to season, the same fish may be found in different parts of the river at different times of the year. Fish need to breathe oxygen like any other animal, but they are able to get their oxygen from the water. In summer the water gets warm and there is less oxygen in the water. Therefore, in the summer, fish are more likely to be caught under waterfalls and *weirs* (artificial waterfalls), or in fast-flowing parts of the river where there is more oxygen. In winter the level of the river may rise because a lot of rain has fallen. When the river is in flood, the current may be too strong for the fish, and so in winter most fish will be caught in the quiet parts of the river. In lakes during the summer the water may get too warm during the day. That is why the best time for fishing often is early in the morning, and in the evening.

● Methods Used for Fishing

Fishing for fun is often called *rod-and-line* fishing. Almost all methods used by fishermen, or *anglers* as they are also called, require a rod and line. The line is wound onto a reel fixed to the *butt* (rod handle). At the end of the line there is a hook. All these things together – the rod, the reel, the line and hook – are called the fisherman's *tackle*. A piece of food, or an imitation of a piece of food, called the *bait,* is attached to the hook. When a fish tries to eat the bait the fisherman jerks the hook into the fish's mouth by suddenly lifting the rod. This is called *striking*. When the fish has been hooked, the line is reeled in to bring in the fish so that the fisherman can take it out of the water. This is called *playing the fish*. It sometimes takes a long time to play a fish, especially if it is a big one.

There are three main methods of fishing. The first method is called *fly fishing*, and is mainly used for Salmon and Trout. The artificial bait, called a *fly,* is made of feathers tied onto a hook to resemble an insect, a small fish or a *nymph* (larva of a water fly). There are two kinds of fly fishing: *dry-fly* fishing and *wet-fly* fishing. In dry-fly fishing, the fly floats on the surface of the water. In wet-fly fishing, the fly is allowed to sink.

The second method of fishing is called *spinning*. In this method the bait is an artificial fish called a *lure.* Different kinds of lures are *spinners, spoons* and *plugs*. The spinner is thrown, or *cast*, into the water. Then the line is reeled in so that the lure moves through the water like a small fish.

The third method of fishing uses real bait to attract the fish. There are several different methods of fishing with real bait. These methods are called *float fishing, ledgering, laying-on, paternostering, upstream worming, live baiting* and the *sink-and-draw* method. If you want to find out more about any of these methods of fishing you can look them up in the A to Z part of this book.

Whatever methods the fisherman uses, he will not catch many fish if he allows the fish to see him. Fish, like most wild animals, are easily frightened by the sight of a man. The fisherman therefore always tries to keep well hidden, especially if he is fishing in a small stream or pond in which the water is very clear. He always avoids stamping about on the bank because fish are very sensitive to vibrations. If the fisherman has not frightened the fish but still does not catch any, he is probably using the wrong bait or the wrong method. But it often happens that the fish prefer one type of bait one day, and refuse the same bait on another day. A good fisherman learns to vary his bait and methods.

Some of the equipment and baits used by fishermen.

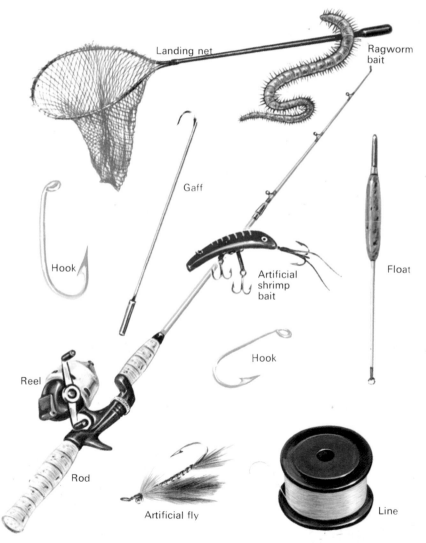

Landing net

Ragworm bait

Gaff

Hook

Artificial shrimp bait

Float

Hook

Reel

Rod

Artificial fly

Line

● Fishing A to Z

BAIT The bait is something that is put on the hook to attract the fish. There are two kinds of bait, natural bait and artificial bait.

For fishing in fresh water there are several kinds of bait. The most common natural bait is bread. This bait can be used in two main ways. The crust is used when the angler wants a bait that will float. Otherwise the bread is made into a paste. It is soaked in water and kneaded until it becomes a smooth paste that will stick to the hook easily. Sometimes the angler will mix honey with the bread paste to make it sweet. Sometimes a coloured dye is added to the bread paste. Other popular baits which are used include worms, maggots—sometimes referred to as gentles—and cheese. Cheese is often very good to use when fishing for Chub. Macaroni, lightly boiled in small pieces, can be threaded on to the hook. For small fish, such as Dace, wheat may be used, and will make a good bait. Insect grubs, such as wasps, are also used. For *dapping* (dropping bait gently into the water), the angler uses grasshoppers, caterpillars or any other insect that can be caught on the river bank. Water weed is sometimes a bait, especially when fishing at weirs. To catch big fish, larger bait must be used. Carp can be caught using lightly-boiled potatoes as bait. For Pike and Perch fishing, small frogs and fish, such as Bleak, Gudgeon and Minnows, are good bait.

There are several kinds of bait used in fresh-water fishing. They include bread and cheese, and live bait, such as maggots and worms.

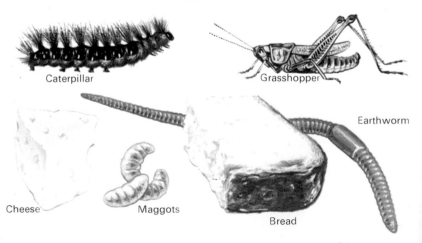

Caterpillar

Grasshopper

Earthworm

Cheese

Maggots

Bread

14

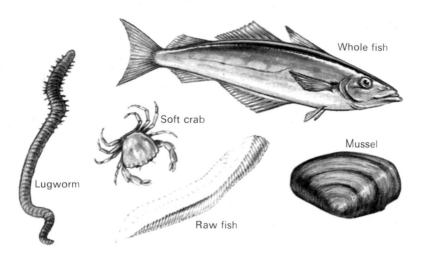

Whole fish

Soft crab

Mussel

Lugworm

Raw fish

The baits used in sea fishing include lugworms that the fishermen dig up on beaches and fish or strips of fish.

Artificial bait for fresh-water fish is of two kinds. The first kind is made to imitate insects. They are called *wet flies* and *dry flies*. The second kind of artificial bait imitates small fish. These baits are called *spoons, spinners* and *plugs*. (See DRY-FLY FISHING, PLUGS, SPINNING, WET-FLY FISHING.)

Natural and artificial bait are also used in sea fishing. Lugworms and ragworms are the most popular natural bait. These worms can be dug up from sandy and muddy beaches when the tide is out. Sand Eels are also used. Small dead fish can be used as bait for larger fish. Small Herrings, Mackerel, Pilchards and Sprats are the best bait. Strips of raw fish, called *lasts,* are also useful. Sea fishermen often bait their hooks with shellfish, especially on rocky coasts. Limpets, Mussels and Razor-fish are good bait, but they must be scooped out of their shells before they are put on the hook. Shrimps, Prawns and small Crabs also make good bait.

Artificial bait for sea fishing is similar to that used by fresh-water anglers. Spinners and spoons are used as well as flies, but they are not made to imitate insects as are fresh-water flies. They are larger and when they are pulled through the water they look like small fish. If real Sand Eels or Lugworms cannot be obtained, a good artificial bait can be made with a thin piece of rubber tube which is attached to the hook. Mackerel are easily caught with large hooks to which feathers are tied.

15

Common baits used for Barbel are worms, bread paste and maggots.

BARBEL FISHING Barbel live in fresh water. They like to live by weirs and in fast flowing water. Barbel feed mainly on the river bottom. The fisherman catches these fish by *ledgering* (fishing with a line fixed to one place). The most common bait is worms. The line needed is a strong one because the Barbel is a powerful swimmer.

BARRACUDA FISHING Barracuda are caught in tropical waters off the coasts of the Americas. They are called 'salt-water pike' because they are very greedy and eat smaller fish. Barracuda are caught by using natural bait or with spinners or plugs.

BASS FISHING There are many kinds of Bass and they can be divided into two groups: salt-water Bass and fresh-water Bass. The salt-water Bass is caught by several methods. When they are next to rocky shores, Bass can be caught with spinners or float tackle. Flies are also used. On sandy coats, Bass sometimes come very close to the shore and can be caught using ledger tackle cast into the waves. This is called *surf fishing*.

The other kind of Bass lives in fresh water. In the Americas there are two kinds of fresh-water Bass called the Small-Mouthed Black Bass and the Large-Mouthed Black Bass. Both kinds of fresh-water Bass are caught with spinners, plugs and live bait. They often live in weedy lakes, and the best way to fish for these Bass is from a boat or canoe.

The Bass is a magnificent fish known for its fighting nature.

Big game fishermen need special equipment to catch many of the powerful fish in the oceans. In order to tire a large fish, which may take several hours, the fisherman is strapped in a 'fighting seat'. This seat is a turntable chair. It has a socket in which the butt of the fisherman's strong rod is held firmly. Big game fish that offer exciting sport include Marlin, Tunny (Tuna), Sharks and Swordfish.

BIG GAME FISHING Sea fishing for very large fish is called *big game fishing*. It has become a very popular sport during the last few years, although it is very expensive. The big game fisherman must hire a motor boat which takes him out to sea where the biggest fish live. After he has hooked a fish, the fisherman is then strapped into a special chair at the stern of the boat. It may take several hours to tire out a large fish. Big game fishermen try to catch Marlin, Tunny (Tuna) and Sharks.

BLEAK Bleak are small silvery fish that live in fresh water. A Bleak is rarely more than 6 inches long, so it can be caught with very fine line and very small hooks. Anglers usually catch Bleak to use as live bait for catching Pike. In France, the scales of Bleak were once used to make silver paint.

BREAM FISHING Bream are caught in slow rivers. They live near the river bottom and are caught by ledgering or float fishing. Bream will take bread paste and worm baits. There are two kinds of Bream. The common Bream is bronze-coloured, and a smaller kind is silvery. Bream also live in lakes.

CARP FISHING Carp fishing is very difficult because Carp are very easily frightened. They live in ponds and lakes and like very weedy places. The fisherman has to use a strong line. There are two ways of catching Carp. One is by bottom fishing with bread paste or lightly boiled potatoes. The bait must be cast a long way away from the bank where the Carp will not be disturbed. Another way to catch Carp is to use a piece of bread which is allowed to float on the surface. Summer is the best season for Carp fishing. Carp sometimes live in slow-flowing rivers.

Two methods of casting: in surf-casting, top, the fisherman swings the rod over his shoulder using his arm and wrist; the seated fisherman, bottom, is casting a fixed-spool reel.

CASTING Sometimes the fisherman can get very close to the fish that he wants to catch. If this is not possible, he must throw his bait to where the fish are. This is called *casting*. There are three ways of casting. The first is called *underhand casting*. The rod is held in front of the fisherman and the bait allowed to swing backward and forward while the fisherman is holding the line. Just when the bait is swinging forward, the fisherman lets go the line and the bait shoots out to where the fish are. For casting longer distances, the *overhand cast* is used. The rod is held up behind the fisherman's shoulder. The rod is then swung over by turning the arm and wrist, just like throwing a stone. *Casting a fly* is more difficult because the fly is very light. The fly fisherman must cast by using the rod like a whip to throw the line out over the water.

CASTING COMPETITIONS Casting competitions are especially popular in America. There are several kinds of casting competitions. One is a competition to see who can cast farthest. This is called a distance competition. All the competitors must use the same weight. Very fine line is used in competition casting because it is easier to cast long distances with fine line. Also, special long rods are sometimes necessary. Another kind of competition is casting for accuracy. A ring made of rubber or wood is floated on the water, and the competitor must try to cast a weight so that it falls into the ring. Distance and accuracy competitions are also organized for fly fishermen.

CATFISH FISHING Catfish are not found in Britain except where they have been introduced. However, they are common in some American and European rivers. Catfish like muddy waters. They are caught with bait made from dead fish. The dead fish is sometimes cut into pieces or sometimes used whole.

CHUB FISHING There are more ways to catch Chub than any other fish. Chub will eat almost anything. Bread paste, cheese, worms, gentles, small frogs and spinners are all good for Chub. During summer, Chub live in the faster flowing parts of rivers. They prefer to be close to the bank in the shade of trees and bushes, where they can dive for cover. In summer, they can be caught by dapping with a grasshopper or caterpillar.

COARSE FISHING There are two groups of fresh-water fish. One contains the members of the Salmon family, and includes the Salmon, Trout, Sea Trout and Grayling. These are called *game fish*. All the other fresh-water fish are called *coarse fish*. The coarse fish are different from game fish because they *spawn* (lay their eggs) at a different time. Coarse fish spawn in the spring. Grayling, however, also spawn in spring. Other game fish spawn in autumn. There are several families of coarse fish. The largest English family of coarse fish is the Carp family. Coarse fish are popular with anglers because they live almost anywhere. You can fish for coarse fish in lakes and ponds, and in many rivers. Coarse fish are more common than game fish, because coarse fish can live in quite dirty water. Very few game fish live in the rivers that run through large towns. The many methods of catching coarse fish include *float fishing, ledgering, spinning* and *live baiting*.

The Cod, which is a popular food, makes good sport for the fisherman.

COD FISHING The Cod is an important sea fish because it is good for eating. In winter, Cod swims near the coast. They feed on the bottom and a common way to catch Cod is by ledgering from the beach. The best time to catch Cod is early in the year.

CONGER EEL FISHING The Conger Eel is a salt-water fish. It is like the fresh-water Eel, but is much bigger. It is very strong and often lives among wrecks and over rocky places. Very strong tackle must be used for Conger fishing.

CRAPPIE FISHING Crappies are a small kind of coarse fish common in the lakes of North America. The fisherman usually needs a boat for Crappie fishing. Crappies are caught with spinning tackle or by using a Minnow as bait.

DACE FISHING Dace are caught in the faster-flowing rivers and streams. Dace can swim very quickly if they are frightened. A single gentle as bait attached to light tackle is good for catching Dace, although some fishermen prefer to catch Dace by fly-fishing, especially during summer.

DAPPING Dapping is a method for catching fish that feed on the water surface. A grasshopper, a caterpillar or an artificial fly is useful as bait. The angler creeps up to the edge of the water and hides in trees or bushes. He holds the rod over the bank and lets out the line until the bait just touches the water's surface. The angler must stay very still so as not to frighten the fish. Dapping is best during the summer when insects often fall from the bank into the water.

DEEP-SEA FISHING Deep-sea fishing is always done from a boat. A common tackle for deep-sea fishing is the *paternoster tackle.* Heavy tackle is used, and the line must be strong but also long enough to reach the sea bottom. Often 300 yards or more of line are used, attached to weights that carry the bait to the bottom. In places where there are strong currents, heavier weights are used. Many deep-sea fish have sharp teeth and are

Having caught one Swordfish, this deep-sea fisherman tries for more.

very strong, so the deep-sea fisherman must use steel *traces*. The *trace* is the bottom part of the line. Instead of nylon, the last ten feet of the line are made of wire, which makes it more difficult for the fish to bite through the line when it has been hooked.

DISGORGER A disgorger is used to take the hook from the fish's mouth after it has been landed. It is especially useful for unhooking fish that have sharp teeth.

DOGFISH FISHING The Dogfish is a small member of the Shark family. It is fished for on rocky coasts, and is quite easy to catch as it will eat almost any bait. Some Dogfish grow to a length of up to five feet.

DRY-FLY FISHING Dry-fly fishing is used to catch Trout and

Artificial flies usually resemble real insects. Top, the Dun and an artificial dun dry fly; below, the Great Red Sedge and some sedge flies.

Dun

Dun Dry Fly

Red Sedge

Light Sedge

Great Red Sedge

Silver Sedge

Cinnamon Sedge

other fish that feed on the water's surface. Many young insects living in rivers and streams come to the surface when they hatch. While the fly is still on the water's surface, it is eaten by the fish. The fisherman imitates the real fly with an artificial one made of feathers. The artificial fly is treated with oil or silicone to make it float. The line must also float, so no extra weights or floats are used. The fly is cast above where fish are feeding and is allowed to float to the fish. The fish mistakes the artificial fly for a real one and is hooked. For dry-fly fishing, the angler needs a very flexible rod with a heavy line tapered at the end. The flies used by dry-fly fishermen imitate natural flies, such as the Mayfly, the Alder fly and the Sedge fly. Because no weights are used in dry-fly fishing, the fly must be cast in a special way. The fisherman flicks the heavy line over his head, out to where the fish are feeding. This kind of casting is very difficult to do if a strong wind is blowing.

EEL FISHING The Eel lays its eggs in the sea, and the young swim to the land and up river. The adult is found in most European rivers and ponds. Eels are caught by *ledgering* or by using a *night line.* The baits used to catch Eels are worms or small dead fish. Thick line is used in Eel fishing because Eels are very strong and can easily tangle or break the line. In some parts of Britain, Eels are caught in large numbers. They are good to eat when jellied or smoked.

FISHING SEASONS Sea fish can be caught at any time of the year. But fresh-water fish can only be caught at certain times of the year. These periods are called *fishing seasons.* Fishing seasons are arranged so that the fish cannot be caught while they are spawning. If fishing were allowed at any time of the year, there would soon be no fish left. The time when fishing is not allowed is called the *close season.* In Britain the coarse fishing close season is from March 15 to June 15. The close season for game fish is different from that of coarse fish because game fish spawn at a different time of the year. The close season for Trout fishing usually runs from the beginning of October until the end of March. The exact dates vary from place to place. The close season for Salmon fishing usually starts in November and finishes in January.

FLOAT FISHING Float fishing is one of the most popular methods of catching fish. The tackle used for float fishing is basically simple, but there are many variations which will be explained later. The bottom few feet of line are called the *cast*. At the top of the cast the float is fixed. (The way in which this is done is explained below, under FLOATS.) Weights are attached to the line to sink the bait. At the bottom of the cast is the hook. When the correct amount of weight is on the line, the float will stand upright on the surface of the water. This is called *cocking* the float. The length of line between the float and the hook is important. If it is long, the bait hangs deep in the water. If the angler wants to fish in shallow water he must shorten the distance between the float and the hook. When a fish takes the bait it pulls the float under the water, and the fisherman knows that he has hooked a fish. Sometimes a fish will swim upwards with the bait, lifting the weights. This causes the float to lie flat on the surface of the water.

In slow-running water or in lakes and ponds a small float is used. Enough weight is used to cock the float. If the fish are feeding at the bottom, the weights are put near the hook so that the bait sinks quickly. Sometimes the fish feed at mid-water; that is, somewhere between the water's surface and the bottom. If so, the weight is put just under the float, so that the bait sinks slowly.

In fast water the float will go downstream, and the fisherman must wind in the line and cast again every so often. This method of float fishing is called *long trotting.* Sometimes a float is used with a ledger tackle. The length of line used between the ledger weight and the float must be at least as long as the depth of the water, otherwise the weight would pull the float under water. This method is called *float ledgering. Live baiting* is a method of float fishing for large fish, in which smaller fish are used as bait. A large float is needed to support the heavy tackle used in live baiting.

A special float is used for fishing in windy weather. An ordinary float bobs up and down when the wind makes the surface of the water choppy. This makes the bait go up and down too, and the fish become frightened. To stop this happening, the angler attaches a float with a large bottom half and a long thin top called an *antenna.* A lot of weight is put on to the line, so that the bottom part of the float is completely under water and is not affected by the waves. As only the thin antenna sticks out above the water, the fisherman can see when he has a bite.

FLOATS Floats are used in most methods of fishing except fly fishing and spinning. The fisherman chooses a different float for different types of fishing. He also varies the float according to the wind and current conditions, and also according to the amount of lead he has put on the line between the float and the hook. In still-water ponds, slow-moving rivers and lakes, a small slender float can be used. Light floats are made from porcupine and bird quills. In faster-flowing rivers, a larger float of cork or plastic is used.

Pike and sea-fishing floats are the largest of all because they must support either live bait or heavy weights that are needed to keep the bait below the waves. Most floats have a small loop made of wire fixed to their bottom ends. The line is threaded through this loop. The float is prevented from slipping up the line by a ring of plastic or rubber. The line is threaded through this ring, which is then fitted around the top end of the float. The top ends of floats are coloured with bright paint so the fisherman can see them easily. The bottom parts of the float are coloured dull brown or green so that the fish are not frightened away.

Fishermen use several kinds of floats. A simple float, left, is far smaller than the big game fish float, centre, for Sharks. An ingenious float for night fishing, right, has a battery-operated light.

FLOUNDER FISHING Flounders are flat fish that live on sandy sea bottoms close to the shore. Occasionally they swim up the rivers where fresh-water fishermen catch them. Flounders are usually caught with *ledger* or *paternoster* tackle.

FLY-FISHING Fly-fishing is mostly used to catch game fish and also coarse and sea fish. Flies are made of feathers and fur. The art of making artificial flies is called *fly-tying*. There are two kinds of *fly-fishing: dry-fly fishing* and *wet-fly fishing*. In dry-fly fishing, the fly floats on the water's surface. In wet-fly fishing the fly is allowed to sink. Fly fishermen have special rods called fly rods, which are more flexible than other rods. They have to be flexible because fly fishermen do not place weights on their line, but instead flick the fly out to where the fish are. To help their casting, anglers use heavy lines. Dry-fly lines are usually tapered, but some lines are of the same thickness throughout.

FLY-TYING Fly-tying is the art of making artificial flies. Some flies are imitations of real flies, but others are lures which just attract the fish's attention. Hooks used for fly-tying have fine shanks. The first part of the fly to be tied is the body. The body is made of silk, fur, feathers or wool which is wrapped around the shank. Sometimes tinsel is also added. Feathers imitate insect wings and legs. An artificial nymph fly does not have any wings because it is a copy of a young water insect. Dry flies must float. Air is trapped between the fronds of the feathers, and this will help to keep the dry fly afloat. Salmon flies are large and often made with brightly-coloured feathers. Feathers from the necks of gamecocks are best for fly tying. These feathers are called *hackles*. The most expert fly-tyers make their flies at the waterside. After they see what flies the fish are already feeding on, they make copies of them.

Flies are also used for catching sea fish such as Mackerel. These flies are easier to make. The angler ties a bunch of feathers around the shank of a hook. These look like small fish when they are pulled through the water.

GAFF A gaff is a sharp hook fixed to a handle. It is used for lifting large fish out of the water when they have been caught. The gaff is hooked under the fish's gills, or through the jaw or side.

As shown above, sea-fishing is often a matter of teamwork. In picture 1, the captain has guided his vessel out to sea and anchored over an area of suitable water. Ground bait has been thrown into the water to attract fish. The fisherman then casts his line into the water and waits. Pictures 2 and 3 show the fisherman reeling in a large Turbot that has taken the bait. Another fisherman waits nearby with a gaff. As the Turbot is hauled out of the water, it is quickly gaffed and pulled aboard. 4 At the end of the day the proud fisherman returns home with his catch.

GAME FISHING The *game fish* are members of the Salmon family. In Britain these are Salmon, Sea Trout, Brown Trout, Rainbow Trout, Grayling and Char. Other countries have game fish, such as the Lake Trout and Land-locked Salmon. The Land-locked Salmon is different from the ordinary Salmon and Sea Trout because it does not go into the sea to feed. Game fishing is very popular because game fish give good sport and are also delicious.

Wet and dry flies are used for catching Trout. Trout may be caught by *upstream worming* (see UPSTREAM WORMING). Salmon are also fished for by fly-fishing. They can be caught by spinning, and sometimes by using worms or other baits. Salmon can only be caught at certain times of the year. Salmon spend most of their lives in the sea, and when they are ready to spawn they swim up rivers, sometimes for many miles. This is called the *run.* It is during the run that the fisherman has a chance to catch Salmon. Sometimes the run may last only a few weeks.

The game fisherman lifts the net and the Salmon is landed.

GAR PIKE FISHING Gar Pike are found in rivers in the southern parts of North America. They grow to a length of eight feet so heavy tackle must be used. Bait for Gar Pike consists of large pieces of fish.

GRAYLING FISHING Grayling are members of the Salmon family, but they spawn at the same time as coarse fish. They can be caught by fly fishing or by float fishing. Bait for Grayling is gentles or small worms.

Grayling are game fish that belong to the Salmon family.

GROUND BAIT Ground bait is thrown into the water to attract fish. There must be enough to attract the fish, but not so much as to feed them too well. Ground bait may consist of bread, worms, or whatever is on the hook. If the water is fast, the ground bait is mixed with clay so that it is not washed away. Sometimes, for Carp and Tench, ground bait is thrown into a pond or lake for a few days before the angler starts fishing.

GUDGEON FISHING The Gudgeon is a small fish. It is caught in shallow parts of slow rivers. The best bait for Gudgeon is small red worms. Gudgeon are often used as live bait.

HAND LINE A hand line is used without a rod when the fisherman can stand above the fish and just lower the bait down to them. Hand lines work best from boats or piers. They are also good for ice fishing.

Sailors once harpooned gigantic Whales from rowing boats.

HARPOON A harpoon is a kind of spear used for catching large fish. It may have several points which are armed with barbs. Harpoons are thrown by hand like a spear, or shot from a gun or a bow. Harpoons shot from a bow are used by fishermen in the South Sea Islands and in South America.

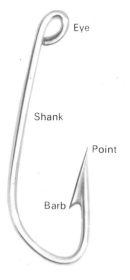

Eye

Shank

Point

Barb

Parts of a hook.

HOOKS A hook is a curved piece of wire. At one end there is a small eye through which the line is tied. The other end of the hook has a sharp point, often with a barb. The barb stops the hook from falling from the fish's mouth. The straight part of the hook, between the bend and the eye, is called the *shank.* Hooks are made in many sizes. The smallest are less than half an inch long, and the largest more than six inches in length. Some hooks are already fixed to a short piece of line. Hooks for catching fish with sharp teeth are tied to fine wire instead of nylon line. Treble hooks are hooks that have three points.

ICE FISHING In very cold countries, rivers and lakes are covered with ice in winter. The angler must first make a hole in the ice, through which he lowers the bait. Hand lines are usually used.

LEDGERING Ledgering is a way to catch fish which feed on the bottom. A lead weight with a hole through it is threaded on to the line, which is fixed to one place. A small piece of lead is clipped onto the line to stop the weight from slipping down to the hook. Up to three feet of line runs between the hook and weight. When a fish takes the bait, it pulls the line through the hole in the weight and makes the tip of the rod jerk. Sometimes fishermen use a float with a ledger to make bites easier to see.

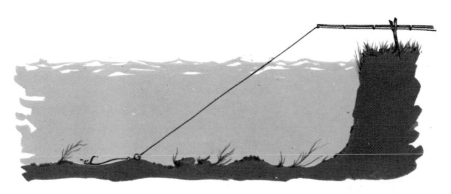

Ledgering is often used in deep water to catch bottom-feeding fish.

LINE Line for fishing was once made of silk and gut, but now it is usually made of nylon. The strength of the line is measured in *pounds breaking strain.* A line of 5 pounds breaking strain is strong enough for most fresh-water fishing. For Pike and Carp fishing you need stronger line. Line of up to 100 pounds breaking strain is used for big game fishing. Line for fly-fishing and float-fishing is *dressed* (treated) with paraffin wax or plastics to make it float. For fresh-water fishing, 50 yards of line is enough. Much longer lines are needed for sea fishing. Often a piece of fine line, called a *cast,* is tied to the end of the main line. A heavy line is used for fly fishing, to make casting easier. For dry-fly fishing, a tapering line is used matching the cast attached to it. This helps the angler to put his fly down lightly.

LIVE BAIT Live bait is good for catching large fish which eat smaller ones. Some fish used as live bait are Bleak and Gudgeon. They can be fixed to the end of the line by a *snap tackle* (a short piece of wire attached to two treble hooks). Live baiting is the most common method for catching Pike.

MACKEREL FISHING The Mackerel is a sea fish. It can be caught in large numbers using hooks on to which brightly-coloured feathers are tied. Other methods for catching Mackerel are spinning and float fishing from a boat.

The Mackerel is a tasty sea fish.

MAHSEER FISHING The Mahseer, a large member of the Carp family, is caught in India. It lives in fast flowing rivers and is similar to the Barbel. Anglers need heavy tackle to catch Mahseer.

MARLIN FISHING Marlin are big game fish, some of which weigh over 1,000 pounds. They are caught by two large hooks baited with strips of fish, sometimes Bonito fish.

A massive Black Marlin is hooked and hauled aboard.

32

MATCH FISHING Many fishing clubs organize fishing matches. Sometimes several hundred fishermen take part. A length of the river bank is marked by numbered pegs. Each fisherman picks a number, and this is the number of the peg where he must fish. Fishing matches sometimes last four or five hours. The fishermen put the fish they catch into *keep nets*. At the end of the match the fish are weighed, and the fisherman with the heaviest catch wins the match. Fishing matches are also organised for sea fishermen, along long beaches or from piers and boats.

MINNOW TRAP Minnows are often used as bait for Trout, Chub and Perch. They are best caught in a trap, such as a bottle with a hole knocked in the end. Bread is put inside the trap. Minnows swim in through the hole and are caught there.

MOUNTAIN STREAM FISHING The angler needs a small fly rod and light tackle for mountain stream fishing. Small Trout are commonly found in streams which are only a few feet wide. *Upstream worming* is the summer method of fishing in mountain streams (see UPSTREAM WORMING).

MULLET FISHING The Mullet is a sea fish, but in summer it is often found in river estuaries. Because Mullet eat almost anything, most bait is good. In harbours they even feed on rubbish tipped into the water from boats. The two main types fished for in Europe are the thick-lipped and the thin-lipped.

Two kinds of Mullet: the thin-lipped, above; the thick-lipped, below.

Fish are kept alive in keep nets which are lowered into the water.

NETS Netting is not considered a sporting method of catching fish. Special nets are used, however, by rod-and-line fishermen. The *landing net,* shaped like a bag, is used to lift large fish out of the water when they have been caught. The net is fixed to a ring at the end of a pole so that the fisherman can reach the fish easily. A *keep net* is a net used in match fishing. It is shaped like a large sock which is hung in the water with the open end above the water. When the fish are caught they are put into the keep net so that they stay alive until the match is over.

NIGHT LINE Night lines are illegal in many parts of the world. They are often used to catch Eels. A hook is baited with a dead fish or large worms and cast into a deep pool. The line is fixed to the bank and left overnight.

PATERNOSTER A paternoster tackle is used to catch Perch and Pike in fresh water, and is also used in sea fishing, especially from piers. A lead weight is tied to the bottom of the line, and pieces of wire called *booms* are also tied to the line above the weight. Booms stick out from the line like arms. Short pieces of line with hooks tied to their ends are fixed to the booms. A paternoster tackle can be used either for live baiting or bait fishing.

PERCH FISHING The Perch is caught with worms, gentles or small fish as bait. Small spinners and plugs can also be used. Perch are common fish found in fast and slow rivers and lakes. A very large Perch, called the Nile Perch, is caught in Africa.

The Perch is a fresh-water fish that is caught with live bait and lures.

PIKE FISHING Pike are caught in most rivers and lakes in Europe and North America. It is one of the largest fresh-water fish in Britain. The Pike feed on other fish. Live baiting was the most common method of catching Pike, but Pike are sometimes also caught with spinners and plugs, especially in America. Tackle used for catching Pike is strong. Wire is used for the trace line because Pike have sharp teeth which easily bite through nylon. The largest Pike are caught in weedy parts of rivers and ponds. They lie hidden in the weeds waiting for small fish. In some rivers Pike are killed by fishermen because they eat other fish.

Strong tackle is used for Pike. Their sharp teeth cut nylon line.

PIKE-PERCH FISHING The Pike-perch is common in Europe. A similar species in America is called the Wall-eye. The Pike-perch resembles both Pike and Perch but is a separate species. The methods used to catch it are the same as those for Pike.

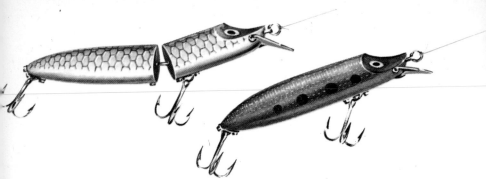

Two kinds of plugs: a double-jointed plug, top; a single plug, bottom

PLUGS Plugs are used to catch Pike, Pike-perch, Perch, Salmon, Trout and many other fish. They are made of wood or plastic. A piece of metal fixed to its front end makes a plug wobble when it is pulled through the water. One or two treble hooks are fixed to the plug. The fisherman casts the plug into the water, then reels his line in slowly. This makes the plug go through the water like a small fish.

PLUMMET A plummet is a piece of lead with a ring fixed to the top, and a piece of cork fixed to the bottom. It is used to find out how deep the water is. The plummet is heavy enough to pull the float under the water. The float is adjusted so that it can be seen at the water's surface after the plummet is dropped below the water. When this adjustment is made, the length of line between the float and the plummet equals the depth of the water.

POLLACK FISHING Pollack are sea fish of the Cod family. They live off rocky coasts and are caught by the ledgering, pater-nostering and spinning methods. Strong line must be used because Pollack are good swimmers.

Pollack are strong fighters often caught over rocky sea-beds.

Centre-pin
reel

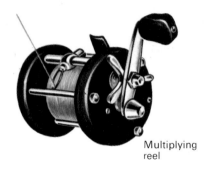

Multiplying
reel

REELS The reel is one of the most important parts of the fisherman's tackle. A reel is always used except when the fisherman uses a hand line or a roach pole. There are three main kinds of reel.

The simplest kind of reel is the *drum reel*. It may be made of metal or wood, and is similar to a cotton reel. The spool turns around a pin which is attached to the frame or cage. It is turned by one or two handles which are fixed to the edge of the spool. The best kind of drum reel is the *centre-pin reel.* This runs very freely and has a *drag*, which is a ratchet that makes it difficult to pull line off the spool. Fish get tired more quickly if they have to pull against a drag.

The second kind of reel is the *multiplying reel.* This reel is similar to a centre-pin reel, but it has a set of cog wheels in its mechanism. If the handle of a multiplying reel is turned round once, the spool turns several times. This mechanism allows line to be reeled in very quickly.

Fixed-spool reel

Three kinds of reel are shown on this page. The centre-pin reel is a drum reel. This reel is similar to a cotton reel. The multiplying reel has cog wheels which make the spool turn several times when the handle is turned once. The spool of the fixed-spool reel does not turn round. Instead the line comes off the edge of the spool.

The third kind of reel is the *fixed-spool reel* or *thread-line reel.* The spool of a fixed spool is fixed so that it points along the rod, not across it. The spool does not turn round. Instead, the line comes off the edge of the spool. If you want to see how a fixed-spool reel works, hold a cotton reel at one end while pulling the cotton off the opposite end. You will see that the cotton comes off the reel in a spiral. It is possible to cast long distances using a fixed-spool reel. The line is wound back on to the spool by a curved piece of wire called the *pick-up* or *bale arm.* This turns when the handle or crank is turned. Because the handle is geared with the pick-up arm, line can be wound in very quickly.

Reels used for sea fishing are similar to those used by fresh-water fishermen. But reels used by sea fishermen are larger because more line is usually needed in sea fishing.

ROACH FISHING Roach are one of the most popular coarse fish of Britain. They are members of the Carp family and are silvery in colour. They are found in lakes and ponds, as well as in fast and slow rivers. Roach eat almost anything except other fish. Some of the bait used for Roach fishing is bread, worms, gentles and wheat. In summer they may be caught using artificial flies. A fine tackle is needed because Roach do not grow to be very large, and big specimens keep away from fishermen. The methods used to catch Roach are float fishing, ledgering, and float ledgering. Roach are often found swimming in large *shoals* (swarms), which is why Roach are often fished for in matches. A lucky angler could catch more than 50 in a day. Small Roach are sometimes used as live bait for Pike fishing.

Roach often swim in large shoals. If the fisherman uses ground baits skilfully, he may catch more than 50 Roach in one day.

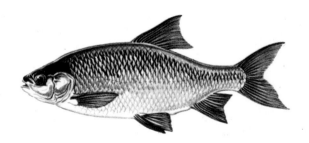

ROACH POLE The roach pole is a rod which is used without a reel. It is longer than most rods used in fresh-water fishing and may be 20 feet long. The rod tip is very flexible, and the line is as long as the rod and tied to the tip of it. The fisherman casts by simply swinging out the line and raising and lowering the rod. The rod is made of several sections joined together. Sometimes it is necessary to take the bottom sections off the rod when the fisherman is trying to land a large fish. The advantage of a roach pole is that casting and *striking* (hooking the fish) can be very quick. Roach poles are used by match fishermen who want to catch large numbers of small fish as quickly as possible. The disadvantage of roach poles is that it is impossible to make long casts.

RODS The rod is the most important part of the fisherman's equipment. Without it, it would be impossible to cast very far. Another important function of the rod is that it helps the fisherman to tire out a fish. When the fish pulls hard the rod bends. This means that the fish must always pull against the springiness of the rod. If the rod is not flexible the line would be broken by sudden jerks made by the pulling fish.

Rods are usually made in two or three sections which makes them easy to carry. The sections are fitted together at the joints by *ferrules,* which are metal tubes that fit into one another. The rod handle is usually covered with cork so that it is comfortable to hold. There are two large rings around the handle that are used to hold the reel tightly on to the handle. Rod rings of various types guide the line along the rod and are bound to the rod by silk thread.

Rods are made of a variety of

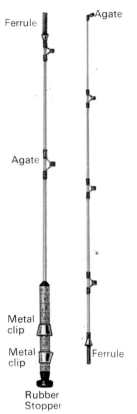

This rod has metal clips for the reel; ferrules to link the rod together; and agates to guide the line.

materials. One material that used to be very common is *greenheart*. Greenheart is a hardwood which is flexible and springy. Once it was used to make all kinds of rods, but now it has been replaced by newer materials. Bamboo cane has always been a popular material for rod making. Some of the best rods are made of split cane. Split cane is made from very straight pieces of bamboo, split and cut so that their cross sections are triangular. Five or six pieces are stuck together to form a rod which has a *pentagonal* (five-sided) or *hexagonal* (six-sided) cross-section. Split cane is very flexible and strong, but it is also very expensive. Steel used to be a popular material for rods, but now most rods are fibre

Types of rods: from left to right: a spinning rod; a fly rod which is good for Salmon and Sea Trout; and a double-handed rod for surf and Salmon fishing. Today rods are made in specially light, tough materials that are easy for young people to handle.

glass. Both solid and hollow tubes of fibre-glass are used. Hollow fibre-glass rods are lighter and more flexible.

For coarse fishing, rods about 12 feet long are used. For match fishing, the rod has a stiff bottom half and a springy top. This permits very fast striking. Stronger and slightly shorter rods are used for bigger fish such as Carp and Pike. For spinning, a short light rod is used.

Fly-fishing rods are usually made of split cane or fibre-glass. They are very flexible so that the line can be cast easily. For Salmon fishing a fly rod up to 15 feet long is sometimes used.

Sea-fishing rods are now mostly made from fibre-glass. They are similar to coarse-fishing rods, but are stronger, especially those used for big-game fishing.

RUDD FISHING The Rudd is very similar to the Roach. It is found in lakes and ponds, but is not common in fast-flowing rivers. The same bait may catch Rudd and Roach, especially bread crust floated on the surface of the water.

The Rudd is a handsome fish that in some ways resembles the Roach.

SALMON FISHING The Salmon is the most important freshwater game fish. It is very popular with fishermen, but it is also important because it makes a tasty dinner. Salmon spend most of their lives in the sea, but are rarely caught there. The Salmon swims into fresh water and spawns in shallow water, often near the river's source. It is said that Salmon do not feed while they are in fresh water. If this is true it is strange that Salmon are ever caught at all! In America and Europe there is a kind of Salmon which never goes to sea. This is called the Land-locked Salmon, and it is fished for in large lakes.

There are many different ways in which Salmon are caught.

In Britain the method used is often fly-fishing with wet flies. Salmon flies are made of brightly-coloured feathers and are not made to imitate a real fly. The fly, which probably looks like a small fish to the Salmon, is cast into the water and the fisherman allows it to float in the current out to the fish. The Salmon is most usually caught when it is at rest. Favourite places where Salmon rest are in deep pools and behind large boulders on the river bottom.

Another method of catching Salmon is by spinning, which is best done in deep pools in rivers below waterfalls. Sometimes the Salmon can be caught with bait such as worms or Prawns. Worms are especially good to use after floods when the water is flowing fast and is dirty.

Salmon leap through this two foot wide throat of water in Scotland.

SHAD FISHING The Shad is a sea fish which comes into fresh water to lay its eggs, like the Salmon. Fishermen catch Shad close to the shore and in river estuaries early in the summer. Shad eat other fish and are caught using bait or spinning tackle. Shad roe (eggs) is considered to be extremely delicious.

SHARK FISHING Shark fishing has become a very popular sport during the last few years. Shark weighing almost 500 pounds have been caught just off the English coast. Because Shark rarely come close to the shore, a boat is necessary. There are several kinds of Shark. The smallest is the Blue Shark. Larger Sharks are the Porbeagle, Mako, and the Thresher Shark. The Thresher Shark will often jump right out of the water when it has

Sharks are attracted by a rubby-dubby, a bag of dead fish.

been hooked, and can swim very fast. One of the largest Sharks is the Mako, which likes the warmer waters off Cornwall.

Shark fishing requires strong tackle. Large hooks are tied to a piece of steel wire up to 20 feet long. A Shark will easily bite through any other kind of line. To attract Shark, a *rubby dubby* is used. This is a sack filled with pieces of dead fish. Any Shark nearby will smell the fish and swim to the boat.

SHORE FISHING Most sea fishing is done from the shore. For deep-sea fishing and big-game fishing, a boat is necessary, but many kinds of sea fish can be caught from the shore. The advantage of shore fishing is that a low tide occurs twice a day. At low tide the shore is not covered with water, and the fisherman can look at the sea bed to see where the rocks and clear stretches of sand are. This is useful information because different fish like different parts of the shore when the tide is in. If the fisherman has studied the sea bed at low tide, he knows where to fish when the tide is in. Another advantage of going to the shore at low tide is that bait can be collected. Lugworms can be dug

The shore fisherman often uses bait found on the beach at low tide.

up from the sand, and crabs and shellfish can be collected from the rocks and rock pools. If this is done the fisherman knows he is using the same things for bait that the fish normally eat. There are several different methods used for shore fishing. Fishing from sandy beaches is called *surf-fishing*. A ledger tackle is often used for surf-fishing. When the fisherman fishes from rocky shores he often prefers to use float-fishing methods because a ledger would get caught on the rocks and weeds on the sea bottom.

SINK AND DRAW Sink and draw is a method for catching Pike and Perch. The bait used is a small dead fish or sometimes, for Perch, a worm, which is then cast a short distance and allowed to sink. The fisherman raises his rod and pulls the bait towards himself for a short distance. The bait is allowed to sink again. The fisherman repeats this several times.

SKATE FISHING The Skate is a member of the Ray family of fish and is related to the Shark. It is a flat fish. Some Skates grow

The Skate, a large, flat fish, is hauled aboard.

very large and strong tackle is needed to catch them. Skates live on the sea bed. The usual method of catching them is by ledger tackle, using a whole fish as bait.

SNAP TACKLE A snap tackle is used for live baiting to catch Pike. It is a piece of wire about a foot long. At the end of the wire is a treble hook. Another treble hook is tied to the wire half-way along its length. This hook slides along the wire so that it can be adjusted to the size of the bait. The other end of the wire is tied to the line. The snap tackle is baited with a small fish about 6 inches long. The bottom treble hook is laid behind the bait's gill-cover, and the other hook is fixed half-way along the bait's back.

SPINNING Spinning is a method for catching the kinds of fish that eat other fish. An artificial fish called a *spinner* is used instead of a real fish. There are several kinds of spinner. One is a *spoon*. A spoon is a curved piece of metal just like the bottom part of a real spoon which is attached to a piece of wire with a hook at the end of it. When a spoon is pulled through the water the curved piece of metal spins round making the spoon look very alive. Spoons are often coloured to make them look even more like real fish. Another kind of spinner is called a *Devon Minnow*. This is about 2 inches long and shaped like a small fish. At the tail end there is a treble hook. At the front there are two

The spoon is a kind of spinner which attracts the fish to the bait.

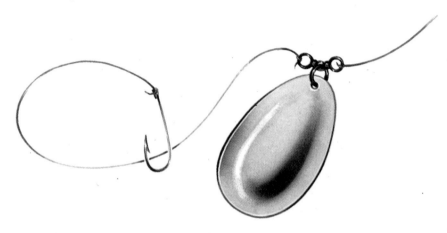

A collection of spinners and spoons.

pieces of metal shaped like a propeller which make the Devon Minnow spin when it is pulled through the water. When fishing with a spinner, a swivel is tied to the line, to which the spinner is attached. This stops the line from getting twisted when the spinner turns.

The rod used for spinning is short and light, which makes it easy to cast a lot without getting tired. A fixed spool reel is usually used, but the multiplying reel is popular in America. Spinning can be a very exciting way of fishing. The fisherman casts his spinner into the water, then winds in the line so that the spinner moves through the water like a fish. The speed at which the line is wound in is important. A good fisherman will vary the speed. When he winds in the line slowly, the spinner will go through the water closer to the bottom. If a fish grabs the spinner it will often hook itself. If not, the fisherman must lift his rod suddenly to pull the hooks into the fish's mouth. Unless the fisherman is quick enough the fish will spit the spinner out, realizing that it has been fooled.

SURF FISHING Surf fishing is done from the sea shore, especially at long beaches. Bait is cast into the waves or beyond them. Often long casts have to be made. To make long casting easier, surf fishermen use long rods and large fixed spool or multiplying reels. Fairly large weights are used in surf fishing because they can be cast far out. Also, a light weight would be

Surf fishermen use long rods so that they can make long casts.

easily washed away by the waves. Surf fishing is an especially popular method for catching Sea Bass in Britain and America.

TARPON FISHING The Tarpon is a large game fish caught in the sea and also in some rivers. It is related to the Herring and grows to a length of 8 feet. It may weigh 200 pounds. The most common method used to catch Tarpon is *trolling*. Once a Tarpon is hooked it may take a long time to land, because Tarpon will swim for miles and have been known to jump 10 feet out of the water.

TENCH FISHING Tench are fresh-water fish that live in muddy ponds and lakes. The best time to catch Tench is early morning in the summer. Tench are not often caught in winter because they lie in the mud on the bottom when it is cold. Worms and bread are used as bait for Tench, because these fish feed on worms as well as weeds, snails and insects. Tench are also found in slow-flowing rivers.

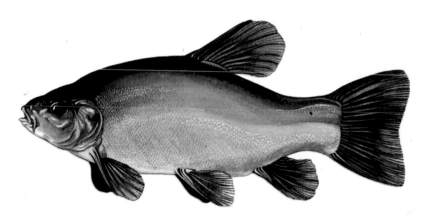

Tench are best caught on early summer mornings.

TRAWLING This method of catching fish is used for commercial fishing, not by the ordinary angler. Trawling is the operation of pulling a large net through the water. The trawl net is about 136 feet long and was once made of twine. But now synthetic fibres are used. Two ships used to work the trawling operation, but now a single vessel with special 'door' designs is used.

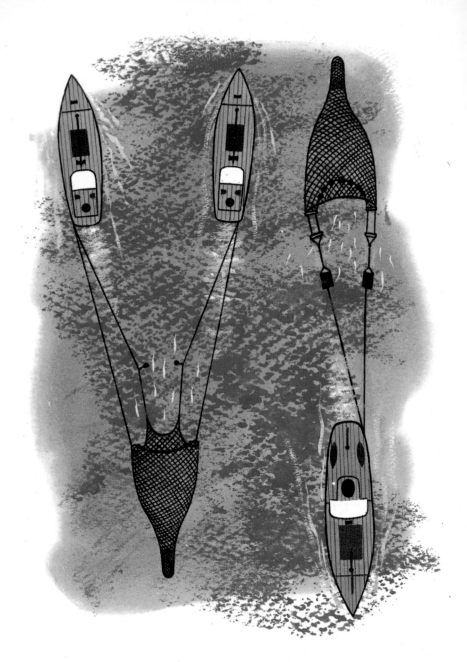

Trawling, an important method used by commercial fishermen, was once carried out by two ships dragging a mid-water trawl behind them. Today only one vessel is normally used. Right, the ship is pulling a bottom trawl.

Trolling or trailing is a rather lazy sport.

TROLLING Trolling is a rather lazy method of fishing. It is done in large lakes and in the sea from a rowing boat. The fisherman uses spinning tackle. Instead of casting the spinner and reeling it in, the troller casts the spinner, then props the rod up against the side of the boat and rows along slowly. A small dead fish is sometimes used as bait. If a fish grabs the bait it usually hooks itself. If a very large fish grabs the bait the rod may be pulled overboard before the fisherman has a chance to stop rowing and get hold of the rod. Trolling is useful when the fisherman is fishing in a new place and does not know where the fish might be.

A Sea Trout, top; a Rainbow Trout, centre; a Brown Trout, bottom.

TROUT FISHING Trout are fished for all over the world. In Britain there are two kinds of Trout — the Brown Trout and the Rainbow Trout. The Sea Trout is really a Brown Trout that migrates to the sea. It is like the Salmon because it spends most of its life in the sea and only comes into rivers to spawn. The Rainbow Trout is an American fish that has been introduced into Britain. In North America, Rainbow Trout are much larger than in Britain, especially those that live in the big lakes. Very large Trout are also caught in New Zealand.

The methods used to catch Trout are described in other parts of this book. They are dry-fly fishing, wet-fly fishing, upstream worming and spinning. Spinning is not a common method of fishing for Trout in places where they are not large. Old Trout eat other Trout. These are called Cannibal Trout and are usually killed if they are caught.

Trout fishing is so popular that in many places the fish are raised on Trout farms. Eggs from female fish and milt from males are mixed in special fish tanks or *hatcheries*. The young Trout are called *fry*. They are fed until they are a few inches long. Then they are put into rivers and lakes to replace the fish that have been caught by the fishermen. This is called *restocking*. If restocking did not take place, Trout would quickly die out in some parts of the world.

TUNNY FISHING Tunny are big game fish related to the Mackerel. They grow to a size of up to 1,000 pounds and are fast swimmers. Strong tackle is used for Tunny fishing and the bait used is usually a dead Mackerel.

UNDERWATER FISHING Underwater fishing is done in the sea. It is especially popular in places where the water is very clear, as it is in the Caribbean or the Mediterranean seas. The underwater fisherman uses a harpoon to spear the fish. The harpoon is shot from a gun which works like a catapult with strong elastic, or with a powerful spring. The fisherman wears flippers on his feet so that he can swim faster and a face mask so that he can see under the water. In shallow water the fisherman uses a *snorkel*. This is a tube held in the mouth so that the other end sticks up out of the water. In deep water the fisherman carries a compressed air cylinder on his back to breathe from. This breathing equipment is called an *aqualung*. Underwater fishing can be a dangerous sport where Sharks or other big fish are common.

Underwater fishing is popular in clear, warm water.

UPSTREAM WORM FISHING Upstream worm fishing is a method of catching Trout in small fast streams. In rivers, the fish always face upstream. Otherwise the water flows through their gills from behind and deprives them of oxygen. Fish facing upstream stay still by swimming against the current. When the angler is fishing upstream, he casts to fish which have their tails toward him. Then there is less chance of the fish seeing the fisherman and being scared. For upstream worm fishing floats are not always used. If the water is very fast, weights are put on the line close to the hooks. The worm is cast upstream and as it is washed toward the fisherman he slowly reels in the line. If the worm suddenly stops coming downstream, the fisherman knows that a fish has taken the bait.

WEIGHTS Weights are used to sink the bait. They are attached to the line, and are of various kinds. The smallest are called *split shot*. These are little balls of lead which have a notch in them. The line is put into the notch and the lead squeezed to close the notch. Larger weights have holes drilled in them through which the line is threaded. In general, if the flow of the water is fast, a bigger weight is needed to stop the bait from getting washed away too quickly.

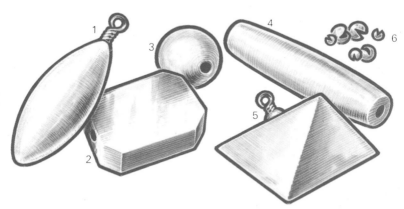

Types of angling weights; 1. Arlesey bomb; 2. Coffin lead; 3. Drilled bullet; 4. Barrel lead; 5. Capta weight; 6. Split shot.

WEIR FISHING Weirs are artificial waterfalls in rivers. Large fish often live in the fast water just below a weir for two reasons. A lot of food gets washed over the weir and the fish wait for it to

Weir fishing is popular because many fish live below weirs.

come to them. Also the water under the weirs is full of oxygen bubbles, and fish need plenty of oxygen to grow quickly. Weir-fishing methods are the same as any other methods used in fast water. Fishermen often use water weed as a bait for weir fishing.

WET-FLY FISHING Wet-fly fishing is similar to dry-fly fishing. The main difference is that the wet fly sinks. It is used to fish for Trout when they are not feeding on flies on the water's surface. It is also the best method for catching Trout in fast-flowing water. Wet flies are tied specially so that they do not float. The most usual method of fishing with a wet fly is to cast downstream and across. The fisherman then works the fly back against the current, taking in line by hand. In upstream casting, the fisherman takes in line quickly, keeping a tight line to his fly in case a fish takes it. The fisherman knows that a fish has taken the fly if the line suddenly stops coming downstream. He can sometimes see the fish take his fly if the water is clear enough. Another kind of wet-fly fishing is called *nymph fishing*. Nymphs are young water insects. When nymph fishing, the line must be treated with wax or floatant so that it floats. Only the bottom end of the cast is untreated, so that the nymph fly floats along just under the water's surface.

Harpoons are fired from guns fixed on the decks of whaling ships.

WHALING The Whale is not a fish at all. It is a mammal because it has warm blood and gives birth to live young. There are many kinds of Whales. Some, like the Blue Whale, are 100 feet long and weigh 150 tons, the weight of a jet airliner. Whales are caught by harpooning. The harpoon is fired from a gun on a large ship. It has an explosive in it to kill the Whale quickly. Whales are hunted because their bodies contain oil.

WRASSE FISHING Wrasse are small sea fish that live along rocky shores. They are caught by float-fishing over rocky places, using crabs and shellfish as bait. Wrasse are usually caught during the summer.

The Wrasse are sea fish that are usually caught in summer.

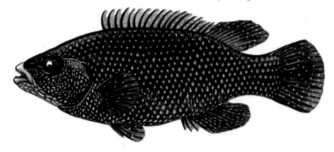

World Records for Sea Fishing (to 1968) ●

AMBERJACK The largest ever was caught by Peter Simons, off Bermuda, in June 1964. It weighed 149 pounds.

BARRACUDA Caught by C. E. Benet, off West End, Bahamas, in August 1932. Weight 103 lbs. 4 oz.

BASS (Californian Black Sea) Caught by Richard Lane, off Catalina Island, California, in July 1962. Weight 557 lbs. 3 oz.

BASS (Giant Sea) Caught by Lynn Joyner, off Fernandina Beach, Florida, in May 1961. Weight 680 lbs.

COD Caught by Joseph Chesla, off Brielle, New Jersey, in March 1967. Weight 81 lbs.

MARLIN (Black) Caught by Alfred Glassell, off Cabo Blanco, Peru, in August 1953. Weight 1,560 lbs.

MARLIN (Blue) Caught by Elliot Fishman, off St Thomas, Virgin Islands, in July 1968. Weight 845 lbs.

MARLIN (Pacific Blue) Caught by André d'Hotman de Villiers, off Le Morne, Mauritius, in February 1966. Weight 1,100 lbs.

MARLIN (Striped) Caught by James Black, off Mayor Island, New Zealand, in February 1948. Weight 465 lbs.

MARLIN (White) Caught by L. F. Hooper, off Miami Beach, Florida, in March 1938. Weight 161 lbs.

SAILFISH (Atlantic) Caught by Tony Burnand, off Ivory Coast, Africa, in January 1961. Weight 141 lbs. 1 oz.

SAILFISH (Pacific) Caught by C. W. Stewart, off Santa Cruz Island, Galapagos Islands, in February 1947. Weight 221 lbs.

SAWFISH Caught by Jack Wagner, off Fort Amador, Canal Zone, Panama, in May 1960. Weight 890 lbs. 8 oz.

SHARK (Blue) Caught by Richard Webster, off Rockport, Massachusetts, in September 1960. Weight 410 lbs.

SHARK (Mako) Caught by B. D. H. Ross, off Mayor Island, New Zealand, in March 1943. Weight 1,100 lbs.

SHARK (White or Man-eating) Caught by Alfred Dean, off Ceduna, South Australia, in April 1959. Weight 2,664 lbs.

SHARK (Porbeagle) Caught by James Kirkup, off Fire Island, New York State, in May 1965. Weight 400 lbs. 8 oz.

SHARK (Thresher) Caught by W. W. Dowding, off Bay of Islands, New Zealand, in March 1937. Weight 922 lbs.

SHARK (Tiger) Caught by Walter Maxwell, off Cherry Grove, South Carolina, in June 1964. Weight 1,780 lbs.

SWORDFISH Caught by L. E. Marron, off Iquique, Chile, in May 1953. Weight 1,182 lbs.

TARPON Caught by M. Salazar, off Lago de Maracaibo, Venezuela, in March 1956. Weight 283 lbs.

TUNA (Allison or Yellowfin) Caught by Henry Nishikawa, off Hanalei, Hawaii, in May 1962. Weight 269 lbs. 8 oz.

TUNA (Atlantic Big-eyed) Caught by Dr Arsenio Cordeiro, off San Miguel, Azores, in July 1960. Weight 295 lbs.

TUNA (Pacific Big-eyed) Caught by Dr Russel Lee, off Cabo Blanco, Peru, in April 1957. Weight 435 lbs.

TUNA (Bluefin) Caught by Dr McI. Hodgson, in St Ann Bay, Nova Scotia, in September 1950. Weight 977 lbs.

WAHOO Caught by John Pirovano, off Cat Clay, Bahamas, in June 1962. Weight 149 lbs.

True Tall Stories ●

LARGEST AND SMALLEST CATCHES. Alf Dean, fishing at Denial Bay, near Ceduna, in South Australia in April, 1959, won fame when he landed the largest fish ever to be caught on a rod. A man-eating White Shark, it weighed 2,664 pounds and was 16 feet 10 inches long. The largest fish ever taken with a harpoon was another White Shark. It weighed 4,500 pounds and was 17 feet long. It was harpooned by Captain Frank Mundus off Montauk Point, New York State, in 1964. A 97-foot-long Blue Whale was the largest marine animal ever to be killed by hand harpoon. It was killed by Archer Davidson in Twofold Bay, New South Wales, Australia, in 1910. In 1955 Don Pinder achieved the distinction of taking the largest fish ever underwater. Off the Florida coast of the United States, he speared a Giant Black Grouper or Jewfish, weighing 804 pounds.

The smallest fully grown fish ever caught is the *Schindleria praematurus*, found off Somoa in the Pacific Ocean. The smallest mature specimens of these weigh only 2 milligrams (about 1/14,000 of an ounce). They are between 12 and 19 millimetres long.

LIVING PREHISTORIC FISH In December, 1938, a living Coelacanth was caught in a trawling net near East London, South Africa. This was perhaps the most surprising catch in fishing history. Previously, this primitive fish was known only from fossil remains. Scientists thought that it had been extinct for more than 70 million years. In 1952, another specimen was found near the Comoro Islands.

LONGEST FIGHT Donal Healey, fishing for a Black Marlin off Tauranga, New Zealand, between January 21 and 22, 1968 set a record for the longest known fight with a fish. It lasted for 32 hours and five minutes. After towing the 12-ton launch for 50 miles, the Marlin broke the line and escaped. The Marlin is thought to have weighed about 1,500 pounds and to have been about 20 feet long.

● Index

Made and printed in Great Britain by Tinling (1973) Ltd.,
Prescot, Lancs. (a member of the Oxley Printing Group).

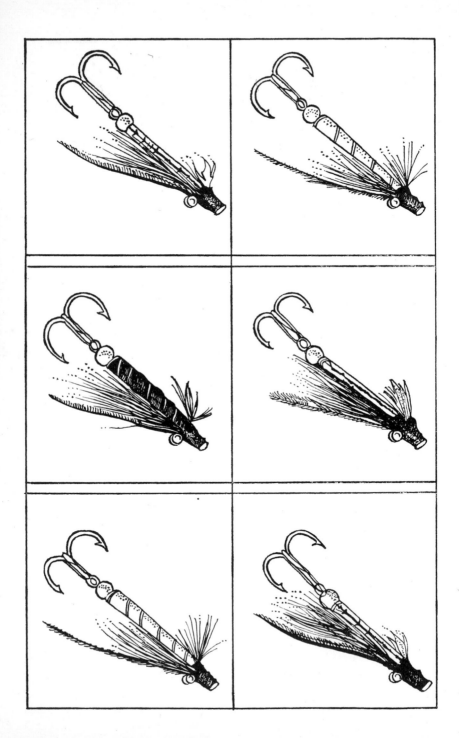